W9-BJS-641

SHAMANS, WITCH DOCTORS, WIZARDS, SORCERERS, AND ALCHEMISTS

ELDORADO INK

The Supernatural

Witches and Wicca

Haunted Places and Ghostly Encounters

New Orleans Voodoo

Shamans, Witch Doctors, Wizards, Sorcerers, and Alchemists

The Undead: Vampires, Zombies, and other Strange Monsters

Legendary Creatures

Unexplained Monsters and Cryptids

Angels, Demons, and Religious Rituals

THE SUPERNATURAL

SHAMANS, WITCH DOCTORS, WIZARDS, SORCERERS, AND ALCHEMISTS

BY DOROTHY KAVANAUGH

ELDORADO INK

Eldorado Ink
PO Box 100097
Pittsburgh, PA 15233
www.eldoradoink.com

Produced by OTTN Publishing, Stockton, New Jersey

CPSIA compliance information: Batch#S2015.
For further information, contact Eldorado Ink at info@eldoradoink.com.

First printing

1 3 5 7 9 8 6 4 2

Library of Congress Cataloging-in-Publication Data

Applied for
   ISBN 978-1-61900-069-8 (hc)
   ISBN 978-1-61900-077-3 (trade)
   ISBN 978-1-61900-085-8 (ebook)

*For information about custom editions, special sales, or premiums,
please contact our special sales department at info@eldoradoink.com.*

TABLE OF CONTENTS

What Is Magic?

In the highest room of a lonely, dusty stone tower, an old man studies an ancient tome intently at a wooden desk. The candlelit room is filled with books, scrolls, and arcane devices; a black raven sits in a gilded cage hanging from the ceiling. The white-haired man is unusually energetic for his advanced age; he is wearing a dark robe and a tall, brimmed hat covered with stars and unusual symbols. A slender wand of yew wood sits on a table nearby. This is the typical image of the wizard, or magician, in popular literature, fantasy movies, television programs, and games.

The word *magic* can be defined as the power to change or influence the course of events by using mysterious or supernatural forces. Magicians, or those who use magic, have been known by many names through history. In prehistoric cultures, religious leaders known as shamans or medicine men were thought to be able to interact with spirits and use magic for healing and protection. In the Mesopotamian civilizations of Sumer, Assyria, and Babylon, people believed their

People who are believed to be able to use powerful magic are called by many names, including shamans, wizards, or sorcerers. Whatever the name, these magicians have been both shunned and revered by societies for much of human history.

Egyptian carving of the ibis-headed god of knowledge and magic, Thoth.

lives were controlled by good and evil spirits they called demons, and that magic could be used to interact with the spirits. The ancient Egyptians worshiped a being called Heka, which was believed to represent a supernatural force that could be drawn on to produce powerful effects. Egyptian magicians called *hekau* chanted spells to protect people, to curse enemies, or to heal the sick. The ancient Persians revered highly educated scholars known as *magi*, who were astronomers and interpreters of dreams and omens. In ancient China, those who used magic were known as *fangshi*.

Although the ancient use of magic generally involved spells, amulets, and interaction with the spirit world, it was considered part of everyday life rather than something unusual or scary. People who were having trouble in their lives or wanted to preserve a streak of good luck relied on magicians to cast spells on their behalf. If the magic didn't work, that didn't mean it wasn't real; that meant some more powerful spell had prevented their magic from working properly.

EVOLUTION OF THE WESTERN CONCEPT OF MAGIC

Some of the most influential traditions related to magic and its application in everyday life were derived from an ancient religious and philosophical tradition known as Hermeticism. This tradition flourished in the lands around the eastern Mediterranean Sea (including Egypt, Persia, and modern-day Turkey) during the second century BCE, after the conquests of Alexander the Great.

The main figure of this religion was a deity or prophet known as Hermes Trismegistus, who blended aspects of an older Egyptian god of magic, Thoth, and the Greek god of magic, Hermes. Hermes Trismegistus did not replace either of these two gods; he was instead thought to be a prophet. Followers of Hermes Trismegistus, who became known as Hermetics, believed that the universe held secret, supernatural powers, and that humans could master and control these powers if they gained enough knowledge. Hermeticism included three main areas that were thought to hold the secret to the universe:

1. Alchemy, the study of material elements and how they are changed through time and other processes;
2. Astrology, which involved the operation of the planets and stars, which was believed to control human destiny; and
3. Theurgy, human interaction with the gods through the use of magic.

Today, a number of writings attributed to Hermes Trismegistus still exist. In them, the prophet instructs his followers about the hidden wisdom, and suggests ways it can be uncovered.

Hermeticism was one of a large number of religious/philosophical systems that developed in the Greek (and later Roman) world between 200 BCE and 300 CE. These systems are collectively known as "mystery religions," because they promised followers a personal interaction with the gods or spirits through the revelation of hidden knowledge. People who were interested in the religion would be initiated into a cult, and they would spend time studying various secret writings in an effort to unlock the mysteries of the universe. The mystery

The word *Trismegistus* can be translated as "thrice great" or "three times great." This refers to what Hermetics called the "three parts of the wisdom of the whole universe"—three areas of study (alchemy, astrology, and theurgy) that could reveal universal secrets to humans.

religions were often influenced by neighboring cultures, such as the cult of Isis from Egypt, the cult of Cybele from Syria, or the cult of Mithras from Persia.

MAGIC AND THE CHRISTIAN CHURCH

Mystery religions were very popular in the Roman Empire, and coexisted with the temples and cults set up to other pagan gods and goddesses, such as Jupiter, Apollo, Minerva, and Artemis. However, in the year 380 CE the Roman Emperor Theodosius declared that Christianity would be the only legal religion in the empire. This led to the mystery religions being persecuted and eliminated by Roman and Church authorities.

A CHRISTIAN MYSTERY RELIGION

Many citizens of the Roman Empire considered Christianity, which developed in the first and second centuries of the common era, to be similar to the mystery religions. There was a mystical branch of the early Christian Church, known as Gnosticism, in which leaders taught that gaining knowledge—particularly a secret or special knowledge—was required for salvation, rather than simply faith in Jesus Christ. (The word *gnostic* comes from the Greek word *gnosis*, meaning "knowledge.") Only those initiated into the highest levels of the Gnostic tradition were allowed to read the secret writings, because the special knowledge they contained was considered too profound or sacred to be disclosed to the general public.

Eventually, mainstream Christian leaders branded Gnosticism to be a heresy, or something that was a false belief, and they actively worked to eliminate it from the early Church.

Once the Christian faith became the official religion of the Roman Empire late in the fourth century, Gnostic teachings were made illegal, and many of the writings were destroyed. Today, archaeologists have recovered around 50 books or fragments of texts, known as the Gnostic Gospels. A large number of texts were discovered at Nag Hammadi, Egypt, in 1945. By studying these writings, modern researchers have gained many insights into the beliefs and practices of people related to magic and its role in religion at the time of the Roman Empire.

Unlike most of the mystery religions, Hermeticism survived this purge. Writings attributed to Hermes Trismegistus were preserved in libraries and at sacred shrines in various places throughout the Middle East. When these lands were later conquered by Arab armies in the seventh and eighth centuries, Muslim scholars translated the Greek and Latin texts into Arabic. Hermetic beliefs were widely known to scholars throughout the Middle East, North Africa, and Central Asia.

After the fall of the western Roman Empire in 476 CE, the Christian Church maintained an influential role in European affairs for more than a thousand years. For much of this period, European civilization was in decline, and most ancient knowledge was lost or destroyed. The only people who received an education were church clerics or members of the landowning nobility. Members of these groups kept tight control over every aspect of European religious and social life. Most people living in Europe were uneducated peasants, who eked out a meager living on small farms and in scattered communities. These people had no access to education, and few opportunities to improve their situation in life.

During this time, the Christian Church taught that the use of "black magic," or sorcery, was evil. Black magic included attempts to harm others with spells, to communicate with spirits of the dead, or to summon demons who would do the magician's bidding on Earth. A

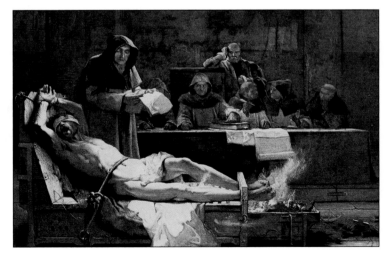

In the Medieval period, the Christian Church often arrested people accused of sorcery. The accused were often tortured until they confessed, and then executed by being burned at the stake.

person convicted by Church authorities of sorcery or witchcraft was often executed.

However, some forms of pagan magic were generally tolerated by the Church. These included folk magic, such as spells for healing people, so long as those spells acknowledged that their magical power came from God or Jesus. Relics of the saints were considered to be like magical amulets that had the power to heal the sick or protect people from harm. Spells and other magical practices were collected into textbooks, called grimoires, which were used by priests and clergymen as well as other educated people during the Middle Ages.

MAGIC AND SCIENCE

During the fourteenth century, Europeans began to gain access to the long-lost writings of the ancient Greeks and Romans, which had been translated and preserved in Muslim-ruled lands. Those writings, as well as other books by Muslim scholars, helped to re-introduce the people of Europe to advanced mathematics, science, medicine, and philosophy, as well as to a wide range of technical, agricultural, and artistic skills. This cultural exchange would help bring Europe out of the Medieval period, ushering in the Renaissance.

During and after the Renaissance, there was a renewed interest in knowledge, and Hermeticism became popular among scholars once again. The idea that humans could use magic to influence or control

A grimoire is a Medieval textbook of magic, which included instructions on how to perform magical spells or create magical objects like amulets. Some books included rituals to summon or invoke supernatural entities such as angels, spirits, and demons.

nature encouraged scientists to explore the magical arts, such as alchemy and astrology. New discoveries were sought, and theories tested with controlled experiments. Most of the scientists from this period who are remembered today believed in Hermetic magic and made their discoveries while seeking proof of its existence.

For example, Sir Francis Bacon (1561–1626), an English scientist and statesman who is credited with developing the "scientific method"—as modern techniques for investigating phenomena, acquiring new knowledge, or correcting errors in existing knowledge are known—was a member of several secret societies based on Hermetic principles.

The Hermetic beliefs of Francis Bacon and other scholars helped lead to many scientific discoveries during the seventeenth and eighteenth centuries.

Another renowned English scientist, Sir Isaac Newton (1642–1727), studied Hermetic writings carefully throughout his lifetime. Notes that Newton kept related to his experiments and scientific work show that he was fascinated by magic and wanted to understand its influence on the natural world. Newton is remembered today for refining Bacon's scientific method, as well as for making important discoveries related to gravity, the movement of planets, and the properties of light, as well as in advanced mathematics.

Many other scientists who made important discoveries in this period, from astronomers like Galileo and Johannes Kepler to the chemist Robert Boyle—owed their accomplishments in part to their interest in magic and the supernatural, and their desire to prove that these things existed and influenced the natural world.

The development of modern science and a general increase in

human knowledge led to a widespread decline in the belief and practice of magic. The period from the 1650s to the 1780s is often called the Enlightenment, or the Age of Reason. During this time many people rejected the idea of supernatural magic that could influence events. Instead, they accepted a new science-based system in which the material world is governed and controlled by the natural laws of physics, chemistry, and other disciplines.

MAGIC IN MODERN TIMES

By the start of the nineteenth century, it seemed like magic might be gone for good in places like Europe and the United States. Yet there were still people who believed in magic and practiced it in secret, and their numbers would grow during the decade. One popular movement, known as Spiritualism, was based on the idea that certain people called mediums could communicate with the spirits of the dead through séances. Although most mediums were frauds, some people remained convinced that the spirit world was real.

In 1887 an organization called the Hermetic Order of the Golden Dawn was founded in Great Britain. The Golden Dawn was devoted to the study and practice of the magic and the occult. Once members were initiated into the organization, they participated in long, complex rituals and ceremonies intended to draw on supernatural powers.

The Hermetic Order of the Golden Dawn inspired many other magical organizations, including one called Ordo Templi Orientis. In the early 1900s a former member of the Golden Dawn named Aleister Crowley (1875–1947) became the leader of Ordo Templi Orientis. He claimed to have been visited by a supernatural being, who dictated the laws of a new religious system called Thelema. Crowley's beliefs continue to have a strong influence on occult practices today. He preferred to use the term *magick* when referring to his rituals, in order to differentiate it from the tricks used by stage magicians and illusionists.

During the early 20th century, there was an increase in the popularity of pagan beliefs, including magic. The term *neopagan* refers to religions that combine many pagan traditions, including magic and belief in a spirit world, but also incorporate some modern ideas. Most

Neopagan religions have become more popular in recent decades. Neopagans perform rituals in order to connect with the spirits and draw on their power for healing or to make changes in their lives.

neopagans believe the natural world contains many deities and spirits, and that humans can communicate with these spirits and draw on their power through magic rituals. Wicca, or modern witchcraft, which was established in the 1940s, is one of the largest and best-known neopagan religions today.

A SCIENTIFIC EXPLANATION FOR MAGIC

Today, people are taught from an early age that there is no such thing as magic, or that belief in spirits or supernatural powers is not logical or rational. Despite this, scientific studies conducted over many years and in many cultures indicate that, even today, many people tend to believe in some type of magic. They may not believe in wizards who cast spells, but people often do have a sense that certain objects, symbols, or rituals have the power to somehow, invisibly, change their life for the better. A baseball player might wear a lucky shirt under his uniform. A housewife might get into the shower in exactly the same way every morning. A child might make a wish while blowing out the candles on his birthday cake. They all believe that doing these things will bring them good fortune.

Anthropologists believe that a belief in supernatural magic may have become ingrained in humans through millions of years of evolution. They note that it is natural for people to give a greater value to certain objects due to their association with another person or to a particular event. One theory that has become popular in recent years holds that this may have originated in ancient fears about illnesses or poisonous food. Prehistoric people did not know what germs were, but they did recognize that a person who ate the same food, or used the same animal-hide blanket, as a sick person was at risk of becoming sick as well. That recognition would have increased an early hominid's chance of survival, and evolution over millions of years would have amplified the characteristic.

As ancient humans became more aware of the history of their food, clothing, and other objects, they began to seek items with positive associations, while avoiding those that had negative ones. People tend to behave the same way today. Many people would feel uncomfortable spending the night in an apartment if they knew someone had been murdered there—even if the apartment had been thoroughly cleaned and all the furniture replaced. At the same time, an ordinary kitchen knife valued at just a few dollars might fetch hundreds at an auction if buyers knew it had been owned by Aleister Crowley. In that case, someone who is interested in magic and the occult would be willing to pay a higher price for the knife simply because of its association with a famous magician.

Scientists say another reason for human belief in magic may be related to what is known as the *post hoc* fallacy. (*Post hoc* is a Latin phrase, short for *Post hoc ergo propter hoc*, which means "After this, therefore because of this.") This is a perception that one thing caused another to happen because it came before the second event, even though the two things may be totally unrelated. For example, imagine a prehistoric farmer noticing that every morning, the sun rises just after his rooster crows. If the farmer didn't know better, he might think that the rooster's crowing actually caused the sun to rise. The farmer might come to believe that if he could find the magic that controlled when his rooster crowed, he could use it to control when the sun rose.

In a similar way, some sociologists contend, when a person thinks about something, and then it happens, the person may come to believe

Renewed interest in magic and the supernatural during the 19th century led to the popularity of "stage magicians," who performed tricks and illusions that seemed to be supernatural by using techniques such as sleight-of-hand. One of the most famous magicians was Harry Houdini, who not only impressed audiences with his tricks, he also spent years trying to show people that the spirit world did not truly exist and that those who claimed to be able to communicate with spirits were frauds.

that her thoughts somehow contributed to, or were responsible for, the event occurring.

Another thing that probably contributes to perceptions of magic and the supernatural is an innate human sense that things happen for a reason. This is an element of many religions, some of them thousands of years old. Yet anthropologists believe that this sense actually stems from one of the most basic of humanity's involuntary physical responses: paranoia.

"We have a bias to see events as intentional, and to see objects as intentionally designed," explains Matthew Hutson, author of *The Seven Laws of Magical Thinking*. "Part of this is because we're always on the lookout for signs of other intentional beings—people or animals—so we tend to assume that if something happened, it was caused by an agent. If we don't see any biological agent, like a person or animal, then we might assume that there's some sort of invisible agent: God or the universe in general with a mind of its own." According to Hutson, such assumptions made prehistoric humans more alert, and this paranoia became ingrained through evolution. So magic and the belief in the supernatural appears to be a part of human DNA, even though it can't be conclusively proven or disproven.

SHAMANS AND WITCH DOCTORS

he shaman remains a vitally important figure in cultures that still follow tribal or indigenous religions. These sort of religions developed in paleolithic times, when human communities were small clans or tribal groups. Their belief systems survived in some isolated areas despite the development of agriculture and the rise of civilizations and organized religions such as Judaism, Christianity, Islam, and Buddhism. Today, it is estimated that more than 250 million indigenous people in North and South America, Africa, some parts of the Pacific Ocean, and Asia continue to follow tribal religions.

There are hundreds of tribal religions, and beliefs and myths can differ widely from place to place. One thing that most indigenous religions have in common is belief in a creator god. This deity is known by many different names. The Algonquian tribes of North America call the creator god Manitou, while the Inuit of the Arctic Circle call it Sila. The Maya of South America call it K'ul. Among the tribes of east and central Africa, the creator god is known as Mulungu. In most tribes, the creator god is depicted as a male authority figure, although

A Peruvian shaman mediates while making an offering to the spirit world in the sacred Urubamba Valley of Peru. In many indigenous cultures, shamans are important religious leaders.

a few matriarchal cultures refer to the creator god as the Great Mother. These are human characterizations, however. All tribal religions agree that the creator god has no gender or age, and is impossible to truly know or understand.

In tribal religions, the creator god is benevolent, having created all the elements that people need in order to live well: good weather, fresh water, game for hunting, and fertile fields for crops. However, this deity generally takes little interest in human affairs. Instead, the creator god employs a variety of spirits that interact with humans.

Ancient cave paintings and pictographs, such as these found in the American southwest, are believed to show evidence of shamans communicating with the spirit world.

THE SPIRIT WORLD

In most indigenous religions, spirits act as intermediaries between humans and the creator god. These religions are animist in nature, which means that the belief system associates divine qualities to animals and objects. In an animist system, natural features such as trees or rivers and creatures like polar bears or coyotes possess spirits that can help humans accomplish their daily tasks. In many religions the spirits of deceased ancestors are also believed to remain near the community. Although ancestors are considered to be less powerful than nature spirits, they can act on behalf of the living by interceding with the creator god to ask for help with problems.

Animism requires a great respect for nature, and indigenous people attempted to live in harmony with the natural world, as this was a way to treat the divine spirits with proper respect. Practitioners of tribal religions believe that the creator god established universal laws to maintain order, and that people can flourish only when they obey these laws. As a result, to maintain the proper relationship with the creator god, humans must understand right from wrong and strive for proper behavior in relation to the spirits. When people violate these universal laws, it disrupts their relationship with both the creator god and the spirit world, and suffering results.

According to tribal religions, nature spirits can inhabit particular places, such as mountains or rivers, and may also exist within wild animals. Their power varies according to the beliefs of the tribe. Some

There are hundreds of Native American, Asian, or African tribal languages. Each language can be used to describe life in great detail, yet none of these languages has a word for "religion." This doesn't mean that spirituality is unimportant to tribal people. In fact, the opposite is true. The spiritual life of most tribes is so rich that it cannot be represented in a single word. Because their religious beliefs are intimately connected to their daily lives, these indigenous peoples have no need to distinguish their beliefs with a separate word.

African cultures believe nature spirits are so powerful they can control the movement of heavenly bodies, while other groups believe that these spirits affect, but do not control, the sun, moon, and stars. Some tribes ask the nature spirits for their help, while others simply regard spirits as a way to explain phenomena of the natural world.

The spirits of ancestors are also important in most tribal religions. Worshippers believe that a person's spirit never dies, but remains in the community, unseen. Living people look to the spirits of their ancestors for guidance in their daily lives.

Because spirits are everywhere, indigenous people feel close ties to the spirits, and believe it is important to communicate with them on a regular basis through prayer and sacrifice. Most indigenous people pray to the spirits every day, expressing gratitude for good fortune, or asking for good health and protection for their family, crops, and cattle.

If a person asks the spirits for rain properly, rain should come. If it doesn't, the person can ask again—this time paying closer attention to the manner in which the request is made. Indigenous people believe that a ritual that is performed correctly will ensure that the spirits grant the request. One mistake in the ritual, however, and the spirits might become angry and refuse to answer prayers.

To keep the spirits happy and make them more likely to grant a request, offerings and sacrifices are often required. Offerings can include food (such as fruit, corn, vegetables, or honey), drinks (such as milk or alcohol), or objects (such as cloth, money, or small tokens). Incense or scented candles may be lit to enhance the offering and make it more pleasing to the spirits. A sacrifice may be required for a more complex request, and generally involves the ritual killing of small animals, such as chickens or dogs. These are then presented to the creator god or to spirits as part of a prescribed ceremony. For some festivals, the entire community may come together to sacrifice larger animals, such as cattle or sheep.

In many indigenous religions, people believe that offending the spirits—whether by accident or on purpose—will lead to suffering. A living person's moral or spiritual misdeeds can damage his or her relationships with family ancestors and with the nature spirits. The mis-

A shaman is responsible for making an acceptable offering to spirits he wants to appease or ask for favors.

fortune is not necessarily limited to the individual who broke the rules; some transgressions can affect the entire community in a nega-tive way, such as causing a drought or a terrible storm. To restore balance and end the suffering, it becomes necessary to repair the spiritual relationship. Generally, individual prayers or offerings are not enough to fix the damage. Serious cases involve the intervention and guidance of religious leaders called shamans.

THE ROLE OF SHAMANS AND MEDIUMS

Those who observe tribal religions believe there is a mystical power—a magic—in the universe. This power is granted by the creator god, and is used by spirits to fulfill human requests. In each society, a few leaders are thought to have an ability to tap into this magical power, serving as the connection between the spirit world and the material world. This ability enables them to heal others, affect weather, and see the future. These gifted religious leaders are often known as shamans.

In North America and Asia, shamans generally interact with the spirit world through rituals in which they enter a trance-like state. They often begin with a period of fasting, or by ingesting certain plants that cause vomiting. Contact with the spirit world is potentially dangerous, and these things are meant to purify the shaman's physical body and ensure his safety. Some tribes will use bells to chase away evil spirits from the area.

Once his body and the ritual space are prepared, the shaman prays and meditates, waiting for a vision from the spirit world that will provide the solution to whatever problem the tribe faces. In some tribes, plants that cause hallucinations, such as peyote, may be used to enhance the vision. Other shamans may undertake an arduous trip into the wilderness, known as a vision quest, in order to receive a message from the spirit world.

Among many Native American tribes, the vision quest was a necessary step toward adulthood. A young man would leave his village and isolate himself in the wilderness for several days. During this time, he fasted and prayed for a vision. Some people gained special powers from their vision quests. The powers could be skill at hunting, or they might be healing powers that would enable them to become a shaman. In that case, the shaman might continue to use vision quests to receive future messages from the spirit world.

Shamans also perform rituals that will enable them to predict future events by interpreting messages found in nature, such as randomly scattered pebbles, shells, or animal entrails. In some tribal societies, particularly in China and Siberia, the shaman would direct the tribe to sacrifice a large animal, such as an ox. Certain bones, such as the shoulder, would be removed and inscribed with a question. The

Many African communities depend on a special type of shaman who is believed to be able to influence the weather due to his relationship with the spirits. The rainmaker's job is to ensure that rain comes when it is needed, and that it stops before crops are ruined by flood. This is accomplished through prayers and rituals performed at certain times of the year.

bone would be thrown into the fire, where it would char and crack. Then the shaman would remove the bone and "read" the pattern of cracks. This would provide information that would enable the shaman to resolve the tribe's concerns.

In Siberia and Asia, as well as in some Native American cultures, the shaman may sing, chant, shake a rattle, or beat a round drum while entering the spirit world. Among the Sami people of Scandinavia, shamans will imitate the sounds of birds and animals in order to call the spirits. Some African dialects are tonal languages, in which the rising or falling pitch of a word changes its meaning. This is also true of aboriginal languages of Australia.

A Sami shaman sits outside his home with a small drum. The Sami are an indigenous people who live in the northern parts of Norway, Sweden, Finland, and the Kola Peninsula of Russia.

Often, the shaman is concerned with the welfare of the entire tribe or community. However, in some cultures the shaman also has an important role in healing individuals. A person's dreams are considered messages from the spirit world, and may hold meaning for that individual or for the entire community. To interpret dreams, the shaman will listen to the dream, and then attempt to dream it himself. In this way the shaman can find a way to resolve spiritual conflicts and help the dreamer.

In some African cultures, a person who is suffering from an illness does not immediately go to the shaman. First, this person must call on a specially trained medium, who can ask the spirits what he or she did to bring on the sickness. Mediums, who are almost always women, allow themselves to be possessed by spirits during special dancing and drumming rituals. By allowing spirits to inhabit their bodies, mediums enable spirits to speak directly to others and tell them things they need to know. Through a medium, spirits may also communicate warnings and desires to the community. This knowledge directs the actions of the community as it attempts to appease the spirit world.

WITCHCRAFT AND SORCERY

The magic of the spirit world is neither good nor evil, and can therefore be used for either purpose. While shamans and mediums use magic to help members of their community, there are also malevolent figures, known as witches or sorcerers, who are thought to be able to tap into that spiritual magic to attack others. Using "black magic,"

The entrance to a Navajo sweat lodge, which was used by shamans to purify themselves before rituals. A sweat lodge is a special hut with heated stones in the center. Water is poured on the stones, creating steam. The steam and tremendous heat would cause the shaman to sweat, which was believed to remove impurities from the body. Many Native American tribes used sweat lodges.

The shaman is often responsible for ceremonies related to people in the community, such as births, deaths, marriages, and coming-of-age rituals. Here, a shaman prepares a six-month-old Melanesian baby for a ceremony called oton, *in which the infant will be allowed to touch the ground for the first time.*

witches are feared to be able to harm a person's physical health, family, crops, or livestock.

When members of an indigenous community suspect that witchcraft is the source of their problems, such as illness or bad fortune, they will often turn to a specialized healer called a witch doctor. Such problems are thought to be caused by damage to the person's spiritual relationship with either the creator god or with a lesser spirit, through the use of black magic. The witch doctor would attempt to heal the person using natural remedies made from herbs, leaves, roots, fruits, tree barks, insects, eggs, or animal parts, and would also cast spells intended to protect the person from future sorcery. People who are believed to be practicing witchcraft are often killed or expelled from tribal communities.

Many followers of tribal religions carry amulets or charms, which are intended to protect them from black magic. The belief that an object has magical powers that can help its owner is called fetishism. This sort of belief is present in other religions, such as Christianity, where some superstitious people carry blessed medals or small relics of the saints for protection.

CONTINUING TRADITIONS

Unlike Christianity and other organized religions, the tribal religions of indigenous people do not have written scriptures or a strict hierarchy of leaders. Instead, traditional practices are reinforced and passed along to younger generations orally, through stories, songs, prayers, and annual rituals.

From birth to death, while hunting or eating or playing games, the spirit world is always present. Indigenous people have felt the spirits from the woodlands of northeastern America to the Andes Mountains in South America, and from the frozen tundra of Siberia to the hot jungles of central Africa. Indigenous tribes have many differences, but their beliefs include many common threads and a similar understanding of magic and the spirits.

An African witch doctor stands outside the hut where he performs healing ceremonies in Mantenga, Swaziland.

WIZARDS AND SORCERERS

The word *magic* is derived from a Persian word, *magus*, that was later adopted into Latin and then English. The word *magus* originally referred to a priest of an ancient Persian religion called Zoroastrianism who was skilled at astrology, or reading the patterns of stars, constellations, and planets in order to foretell the future. The *magi* (the plural form of magus) used their knowledge of the planets and stars to set the proper dates for solstices and equinoxes. These dates were important to ancient cultures not only as religious festivals, but on a more practical level as well. Knowing exactly when the seasons began helped farmers choose the best times to plant or harvest their crops.

The Persian magi were wise and respected, and their practices were unusual and hard for common folk to understand. To ordinary, uneducated people, their work seemed like magic, and the magi were both respected for their knowledge and feared for their power. The same has been true of practically all magicians, wizards, or sorcerers throughout human history.

MAGICIANS IN THE ANCIENT WORLD

More than 8,000 years ago tribal groups began to organize and develop civilizations in Mesopotamia, Egypt, the Indus Valley, and China. These civilizations were characterized by the development of agricul-

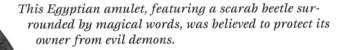

This Egyptian amulet, featuring a scarab beetle surrounded by magical words, was believed to protect its owner from evil demons.

ture, the domestication of animals, the development of writing, and, eventually, the use of tools and weapons made from metals like copper or bronze. These early civilizations also featured the first organized state religions. Many of these religions featured pantheons of gods and goddesses, each of whom was considered to be responsible for certain natural functions, such as storms or the movement of the sun. In some places, such as Mesopotamia and Egypt, enormous temples and monuments were built to honor the gods. The shamans of tribal religions were replaced by priests, religious leaders who cared for the temples and shrines to specific deities.

According to archaeological records found in the ancient cities of Mesopotamia and Egypt, people believed that spirits they called demons had a strong effect on their lives. The demons could work for either good or evil. Priests and magicians studied the demons and sought ways to communicate with them. They created amulets and cast spells intended to influence the demons. Many of these spells have survived. They were written on papyrus scrolls found in Egyptian tombs, or carved onto clay tablets in Mesopotamian libraries.

The Hebrew Bible (or Christian Old Testament), which was written about 3,500 years ago, includes numerous mentions of magic and those who practice it. The Book of Exodus describes how God tells the Israelite leader Moses and his brother Aaron to engage in a battle with magicians in the Egyptian Pharaoh's court. To demonstrate their magical power, both Aaron and the Pharaoh's magicians turn their wooden staffs into snakes. However, Aaron's snake devours the other snakes, showing that God's power is greater than that of the court magicians, who are aided, presumably, by supernatural demons.

Later, after God strikes Egypt with a series of plagues, the Pharaoh allows Moses and the Israelites to leave Egypt. The Israelites then wander through the desert for forty years, looking for a place to settle. At one point the Israelites encounter a powerful magician named Balaam. The Book of Numbers describes how the king of Moab hires Balaam to cast a spell on the Israelites so they won't invade his land. Balaam finds himself without the magical power to curse the Israelites, and God orders him to bless them instead. Balaam then returns to the king of Moab, and predicts that a great Israelite king will one day conquer Moab and the neighboring kingdom of Edom. This predic-

The Greek mathematician Pythagoras of Samos, who lived in the fifth century BCE, *was believed to be a powerful magician.*

tion concerns the rise of Israel's King David, who would come to power some 500 years after Moses and consolidate power in the region known as Palestine.

Around the year 1,000 BCE, David and his son Solomon established the kingdom of Israel as a regional power. However, over time Israel grew weaker. The northern half of the kingdom was conquered by the Assyrians in 722 BCE; the southern half, known as Judah and based in Jerusalem, remained independent, but was eventually conquered by the Babylonians. The Jewish people were taken into captivity in Babylon around 586 BCE.

According to the Biblical Book of Daniel, one of those taken to Babylon was a young man named Daniel. He and several other intelligent young Jews were educated at the court of the Babylonian ruler, so they could serve as advisors to the king, Nebuchadnezzar.

This carving of the three Magi presenting their gifts to the infant Jesus ornaments the church of Saint Antione in Brussels.

Like other civilizations of ancient Mesopotamia, the people of Babylon were interested in astrology and magic. Royal magicians cast spells and practiced divination, in order to predict future events and figure out the secrets of the supernatural world. But when Nebuchadnezzar has a dream that none of the magicians can understand, Daniel is the only one able to explain its meaning to the king. "No wise man, enchanter, magician or diviner can explain to the king the mystery he has asked about, but there is a God in heaven who reveals mysteries," Daniel says, explaining that his powers come from God, not supernatural magic.

MAGIC IN THE ROMAN EMPIRE

The Bible also provides information on the use of magic in the Roman Empire. One of the most famous references occurs near the start of the Gospel of Matthew. That account of Jesus's birth says that the Magi, or wise men, from the East follow a star to the town of Bethlehem, where Jesus has been born. When the Magi find Jesus, they honor him with gifts of gold (representing kingship and royal power), frankincense (a type of incense that was used by priests, signifying religious authority), and myrrh (an oil used to anoint and prepare dead bodies before burial, representing what Christians believe is Jesus's ultimate purpose on Earth, to die for the sins of humankind).

In the New Testament book Acts of the Apostles, which was written in the first century CE, a character named Simon Magus is said to be a powerful magician who amazes the people of Jerusalem with his works. Simon is impressed by the apostles' ability to heal people and cast out evil spirits. He offers to pay Peter and John if they will sell him the secret of their magical ability. His offer is rejected, and the apostles explain that their power comes from God, not magic. In other ancient writings, Simon Magus is killed when his magic fails him during a battle with the apostles.

Another story from Acts of the Apostles tells of the Apostle Paul preaching in the town of Ephesus, in modern-day Turkey. The apostle's healing ability impresses so many people that they decide to follow Jesus. Acts 19 says that many people who had practiced sorcery brought out their scrolls containing spells and burned them publicly.

The Christian scriptures, as well as other sources, indicate that Roman authorities accepted the use of magic. Magicians in the provinces of Rome were permitted to use spells to resolve individual problems related to love, sickness, and everyday life. However, sorcery—magic meant to harm or kill people, or to destroy property—was usually illegal. So was necromancy, the use of magic to communicate with the spirits of dead people. Existing Roman records document the trials and executions of those who practiced sorcery or necromancy.

One form of magic that seems to have been acceptable in the Roman Empire was the use of curse tablets. Magicians would prepare

This thin sheet of gold is inscribed with Greek letters and magical symbols. It contains a spell intended to help a man named Proclus win a trial in the Roman province of Arabia. It ends with a curse on his opponents, whom he wishes silenced, subjugated, and enslaved.

small sheets of flattened metal, such as lead, tin, copper, or even gold, that were inscribed with a spell. Many of the curse tablets contain grievances or requests that an enemy be punished by the gods. Other tablets contained prayers, requests for good luck, and even love spells. Thousands of these tablets have been excavated from Roman ruins.

Romans historians wrote about the magicians of other cultures that they encountered. In the British Isles, on the frontier of the Empire, the Romans fought with a Celtic people led by the Druids. According to the Roman author Pliny the Elder, the Druids were educated in astronomy and astrology. They worshiped nature, and used their magic spells and rituals to predict the future. Most practices of the Druids are unknown, but they were probably similar to other pagan religions of the time.

To the North of the Roman Empire, the Germanic tribes who lived in Scandinavia and northern Europe believed that magicians known as völva could predict the future and cast spells. The völva were usually unmarried older women, and they traveled throughout the country accompanied by assistants. They would sell their magical services to those who needed them. Völva used wands and other tools in their magic. They were so respected that, according to Norse mythology, the most important god, Odin, once visited a völva for advice about future events that would affect the gods.

Origins of the Wizard

The word *wizard* comes from an Old English word *wys*, meaning "wise." As the name indicates, the original wizards were people who were older and were well-educated. Some wizards may have studied magical arts, such as astrology or alchemy. Often, wizards served as advisors to the ruler, and may have been expected to predict a good course of action in times of crisis or war.

The most famous Medieval wizard from Britain is the legendary Merlin, who is associated with tales about King Arthur and his court. The magician character from the tales was created by Geoffrey of Monmouth in the twelfth century. He based Merlin on several real-life figures from Welsh history.

Other writers would expand on the Arthurian legend, adding stories about Merlin and his magic. Among the best known of these works was Sir Thomas Malory's *Le Morte d'Arthur* (1485). Merlin appears as a relatively minor character in some of the stories, but another magician plays a more malevolent role—the sorceress Morgan le Fay, who is partly responsible for Arthur's death.

The fictional wizard Merlin became the archetype for the magician in Medieval literature—a wise old man who acts as a mentor to a young ruler.

Many of the Medieval wizards made no claim to magical powers. Among the most famous of them was a German bishop named Albertus Magnus (1200–1280), who was one of the most learned men of his time. In addition to theology, Albertus studied alchemy and astrology, and he conducted many science experiments. In his writings, Albertus tried to harmonize what he had learned from his experiments and studies of nature with Christian teachings.

Although he was often called a wizard, there is no evidence that Albertus Magnus was involved in magic or occult practices. Clearly the Church had no concerns, for after Albertus's death he was canonized as a saint. However, due to his reputation as a scholar, after his death some writings about magic and alchemy were falsely attributed to Albertus. As a result he is often incorrectly identified as a sorcerer.

Another clergyman who was considered a wizard was Roger Bacon (1214–1292), an English friar who, like Albertus, wrote extensively about science and how it related to Christian theology. Interestingly, one of his books was written specifically to dismiss the idea of supernatural magic, although it did include some useful information for alchemists. According to legends, Bacon created a mechanical brass head that could answer any question it was asked.

MEDIEVAL SORCERERS

The danger of being an educated person or a scientist during the Medieval period was that, if you wrote something that went against the teachings of the Christian Church, you were likely to be accused of being a sorcerer, or someone who practiced black magic. Sorcerers were believed to be servants of the Devil, and their magic came from demons in order to do evil things in the material world. Sorcerers were blamed for many bad things that occurred, including wars, storms, and plagues.

Beginning in the twelfth century, the Christian Church implemented a new program throughout Europe called the Inquisition. Its purpose was to identify those who held beliefs that Church leaders thought posed a threat to their religious teachings. Those arrested by the Inquisition were often tortured until they admitted to crimes. Those punished by the Inquisition included people who were suspected of devil worship or accused of practicing sorcery.

There certainly were some people who wished to learn more about magic in order to gain power or revenge, or to fulfill sadistic desires. One infamous Medieval sorcerer was a French nobleman named Gilles de Rais (1405–1440). He was a respected military leader who had fought with Joan of Arc against the English during the Hundred Years War, and retired as one of the highest-ranking generals in France. However, after retiring his personality changed dramatically. He began to study the occult intensely, and performed numerous ceremonies hoping to summon a demon that would make him wealthy.

In some countries, people are still executed for performing magic. For example, it is estimated that about 200 people are convicted and executed in Saudi Arabia each year for engaging in sorcery or witchcraft. In 2014, for example, a 60-year-old woman was executed because she had been paid about $800 by several people in hopes that she could heal them from sickness. Foreign visitors have been charged with witchcraft for bringing family heirlooms to the country that Saudi authorities believe are magical amulets.

However, despite his preparations—which included the murder of a child to be offered as a sacrifice to the demon—his spells failed to work. Eventually, when Gilles de Rais was arrested, investigators discovered that he had killed more than 80 people, making him one of history's first serial murderers. He was executed for his crimes.

Another person executed by the Inquisition for sorcery was Giordano Bruno (1548–1600), an Italican cleric who had studied Hermetics and wrote books disagreeing with Church doctrine about astronomy. Bruno was accused of engaging in the use of magic, among other crimes, and was burned at the stake.

WIZARDRY TODAY

Today, the word *wizard* is often used to refer to someone who is exceptionally good at something. A person might be a wizard (or a "whiz," for short) with a computer or on the basketball court. Hall of Fame shortstop Ozzie Smith was known as The Wizard because of his amazing defense on the baseball diamond. The word does not have as much of a connotation with supernatural magic; instead, it refers to an innate ability to make things happen in a positive way.

Some people who practice New Age or neopagan religions call themselves modern-day wizards. New Age religions combine many traditions and call on both old and new ideas, from magic to astrology, crystal healing, meditation, and alternative medicine. Neopagan religions are based on ancient pagan practices, including worship of nature and the spirit world. In general, these religions share an ancient belief that the natural world is bound together by a powerful energy force, which is unseen yet connected to all living things. They believe that if they are in proper balance with that force, they have the power to make changes in their lives, as well as in the lives of others. Modern wizards may not shoot fire from their fingertips or change into birds or animals, However, they believe that they are capable of performing rituals or casting spells that will enable changes to begin in another person's life.

ALCHEMISTS

Did you bring what I need," the old man hissed, using bellows to stoke a small fire while glaring at the person who had entered his chamber. The visitor nodded. "Bring it here," said the old man, hand outstretched to receive the small vial of mercury that the visitor carried. Examining the silvery liquid, he carefully added a few drops to a small clay crucible simmering over the fire. "And now, the vital ingredient," the old man explained, as he added several grains of white powder to the mixture. "We shall see if, this time, our experiment is a success!"

This is the image most people have of the alchemist, a type of magician that was well known in the Medieval period. According to Hermetic teachings, alchemy was one of the three areas where the wisdom of the universe could be uncovered through serious study.

WHAT IS ALCHEMY?

In many ways, alchemy can be considered a forerunner of a legitimate contemporary scientific discipline—chemistry, which is the study of

This seventeenth-century painting shows a Medieval alchemist using bellows to heat a small fire under the crucible in which he hopes to turn a base metal into gold.

A statue of the Greek philosopher Aristotle, who is sometimes called the world's first scientist. His writings on the properties of the material world had a great influence on later scholars.

the composition, structure, and properties of matter, and how different atoms and molecules change when they interact with other atoms or molecules. Like modern chemists, alchemists were interested in the transformation of matter. The "scientific theories" behind alchemy, however, were based on a faulty understanding of the Earth and its elements in ancient and medieval times.

During the fourth century BCE, the great Greek philosopher Aristotle taught that all physical matter is composed of four elements—earth, air, water, and fire. The nature of that matter—whether it is a person, a peacock, or a planet—is determined by the balance of the elements within it.

Aristotle and other Greek philosophers also taught that there was an order to everything in the universe, including the planets and stars. They believed that the Earth was at the center of the universe, and was circled by the stars and the seven known planets. (Five of these were the actual planets we know as Mercury, Mars, Venus, Jupiter, and Saturn; the ancients believed that the Sun and Moon were also planets.) Aristotle developed a system of circular orbits for the stars and planets around the Earth.

Today, people understand that the Earth is not the center of the universe, and that it orbits the Sun, as do the other planets in our solar system. However, because Aristotle's system, which is called a geocentric model, could accurately describe the movement of heavenly bodies to an observer on Earth, it was widely believed to be correct in his time, and remained the predominant view of the universe for roughly eighteen centuries.

In Europe and Western Asia, Aristotle's model of the universe, along with his thoughts about order and organization, were endorsed by the Christian church because they aligned with Biblical teachings. Just as the church believed in a hierarchy of Heaven, with various levels of angels and created beings, so the universe was arranged in a divine order, ascending from the imperfect to the pure. The Church taught that over time, coarse and imperfect matter would eventually be refined and changed into a pure state—just as humans, after death and God's judgement, would be "perfected" and live in a pure state in Heaven.

Medieval alchemists believed that there were seven metals, each corresponding to one of the seven known planets: lead for Saturn, tin for Jupiter, copper for Venus, iron for Mars, mercury for Mercury, silver for the Moon, and gold for the Sun. In the normal order of things, these metals would, over time, be refined naturally into a purer form. Iron would become mercury, mercury would become silver, and so on. Eventually, at the end of time, all metals would have transformed into gold, the purest substance and what the heavens were made of.

These pages from a Medieval atlas show the Earth at the center of the universe, ringed by zodiac symbols. Alchemists believed that the order and organization shown by the stars and planets, which moved through the sky in predictable ways, was a characteristic of all Earthly matter as well. This worldview indicated that transmutation of elements was possible.

The goal of the alchemists was to find a way to hasten this natural process—to change a less valuable metal into its pure gold form. To do this, alchemists sought a magical substance known as the philosopher's stone. According to ancient legends, the philosopher's stone was a substance that could turn "base metals," or common, inexpensive elements like lead, copper, or iron, into "noble metals," or precious elements like gold or silver. The philosopher's stone was not actually a stone; it is usually described as a white powder.

Some alchemists sought transformation of humans, rather than metals. The believed there was an elixir that would act like the philosopher's stone. If properly mixed or applied, this elixir would speed up the natural refinement of human beings, providing longevity, then immortality and, finally, redemption as a pure being.

SEEKING SCIENTIFIC KNOWLEDGE

Today, the word "alchemy" has a generally negative connotation. Many people consider it a pseudo-science that was practiced by scam artists, who sold fake formulas to greedy dupes hoping to turn ordinary lead into a golden fortune. However, during the Medieval period most people believed alchemy was a legitimate branch of science. It was hard, in fact, to distinguish the experiments of alchemists from legitimate work in other scientific fields, such as metallurgy. In Medieval and Renaissance Europe, many scholars who made important scientific discoveries were also involved in alchemy.

For example, Tycho Brahe (1546–1601), a Danish scientist who is known today for his studies on the movement of the stars and planets, spent much of his life pursuing alchemy. He was such a famous scientist that during the 1570s, King Frederick II of Denmark built a special facility for him on the island of Hven. The building had an observatory, for studying the stars, on the upper level, and a laboratory on the lower level where he could conduct experiments in alchemy. The facility, called Uraniborg, was a research center that employed nearly 100 students and artisans for the next two decades.

The Polish doctor and alchemist Michael Sendivogius (1566–1636) wrote several books about magic and alchemy. However,

The word alchemy has its origins in an Arabic word, al-kimiya, *which meant "philosopher's stone." During the eighth and ninth centuries, Arabic scholars translated and studied the works of ancient Greek philosophers and conducted their own studies into the physical properties of matter. During the later Medieval period, European scholars gained access to the scholarship of the Muslims on alchemy, which fueled interest in the discipline.*

he is best remembered today for identifying oxygen, and distilling it in a lab in Kraków sometime around 1600. He also worked with acids and other chemical compounds.

Jan Baptist van Helmont (1580–1644) is thought to be the first scientist to understand that the air is composed of many different gases. In fact, the Belgian alchemist invented the word "gas" and introduced it into subsequent scientific discussions. Van Helmont was the first to identify carbon dioxide, which he called "gas sylvestre," and he conducted many other experiments.

Most experts consider Robert Boyle (1627–1691) to be the first modern chemist. Boyle had a lifelong interest in alchemy, and this was

Sir Isaac Newton was one of the leading figures of the scientific revolution. After his death, notes in his journals indicated that Newton had secretly been an avid practitioner of alchemy. Newton believed in Hermetic magic, and hoped that through his studies he could unlock the secrets of the universe.

the basis for most of his experiments. He was widely respected in his time, and was among the first people appointed to the Royal Society of London for Improving Natural Knowledge, a scientific organization of leading scientists and inventors established by England's King Charles II. Today, he is known best for Boyle's Law, which is related to the properties of gas, as well as for a number of the methods he developed to carry out experiments.

Just like Isaac Newton and other scientists of this time, Brahe, Sendivogius, van Helmont, and Boyle were all Christians who also accepted Hermetic ideas about magic that were permitted by the Church. Rather than interfering in their studies, belief in magic helped lead to their practical achievements in medicine and science.

Other alchemists made notable discoveries that today are used in chemistry and other sciences. These include some basic chemical procedures, such as distillation, which purifies liquids through a process of heating and cooling. Distillation was first done by Greek alchemists roughly 2,000 years ago. Another procedure used today is fractional distillation, which involves separating a mixture into separate chemical compounds by heating them. This process was recorded by an Italian alchemist in 1540. During the 16th century, alchemists also discovered several elements, such as phosphorus, antimony, and bismuth, that must be extracted from mineral ores. Alchemists also learned how to prepare and use nitric acid, hydrochloric acid, and sulphuric acid. These are essential parts of many chemical reactions today.

FRAUDULENT ALCHEMISTS

The idea of creating gold from inexpensive materials represented a potential get-rich-quick scheme that was very appealing to greedy and gullible people. As a result, many self-described alchemists were really con men who were happy to sell a magic potion, or their "recipe" for the philosopher's stone, to a sucker, escaping with the money before the greedy person could discover that the formula did not work.

Fraudulent alchemists used many tricks to fool their clients. One method involved preparing a crucible with a false bottom. The con man would hide some small bits of gold beneath the false bottom, which was often made from a metal with a low melting point. When the phony alchemist wanted to show that his philosopher's stone worked, he would place some base metal like copper or lead into the crucible, along with various substances claimed to have mystical powers (the more the better, to mystify the sucker) and of course the magic powder (which might be ground-up chalk or something similar in appearance). Heating the crucible in a furnace would cause the false bottom to melt, revealing the gold so that it would be found once the mixture cooled.

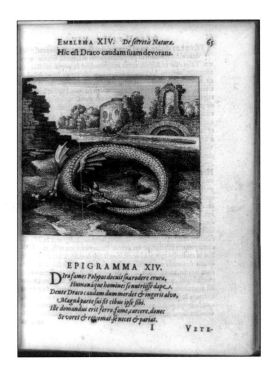

Alchemy had its own terminology, which used special language and symbols. Often messages were written in code, or encrypted into stories or puzzles, to keep the alchemist's notes safe from others. This illustration from a book on alchemy, published in 1618, shows a dragon biting its own tail. This was a common alchemical symbol, known as the ouroboros. It represents something that is cyclical, such as the seasons of the year. An ouroboros can also be seen in the magical amulet on page 30.

Even the great scientist Robert Boyle was once duped by a con man. In 1677, a Frenchman named Georges Pierre des Clozets contacted Boyle. He told the scientist that he represented a secret society of alchemists called The Asterism. According to Pierre, the society possessed the answers to many of the problems that Boyle was seeking to understand through his experiments. Pierre offered to help Boyle become a member of The Asterism, promising that once he joined he would have access to the group's secret knowledge. For more than a year, Pierre strung Boyle along, receiving money and expensive gifts from the scientist in return for the work he was doing to get Boyle admitted to the society. In 1678, Pierre disappeared. Boyle soon learned, to his embarrassment, that there was no such organization as The Asterism.

Another alchemist con man was Giuseppe Balsamo (1743–1795). Although born to a poor family in Sicily in the eighteenth century, he would reinvent himself as an Italian nobleman, Count Alessandro di Cagliostro. He traveled across Europe, promoting himself as a healer, mystic, and alchemist. Cagliostro claimed to be able to speak with the dead and cast out demons. He sold the elixir of life and the philosopher's stone to gullible people. Cagliostro was charismatic and gained many followers, while interacting with such famous figures as Russian ruler Catherine the Great, the German writer and statesman Johann Wolfgang von Goethe, Austrian composer Wolfgang Amadeus Mozart, French queen Marie Antoinette, and English poet and mystic William Blake. Cagliostro was captured in 1789, and imprisoned by the Inquisition for his crimes. He died in prison six years later.

Medieval alchemists never managed to turn base metals into gold. However, modern-day physicists have been able to create gold atoms by exposing substances like platinum or mercury to radiation. Unfortunately, the mass of the gold atoms created through this process is extremely small—so small that if the reaction could be maintained for 50 million years, only one gram of gold would be produced!

Because of the many scams and con men, in some areas alchemy was declared illegal. In other places, it could be practiced only with permission from the local ruler.

European rulers had good reasons for wanting to control alchemists. If someone did succeed in creating gold cheaply, it could destabilize their kingdom's economy. Additionally, alchemists believed that if they found the philosopher's stone they would gain power to change anything in the natural world, not just base metals into a purer form. That sort of power would be of great interest to a ruler. They could afford to sponsor alchemists to work exclusively for their kingdom, and

Carl Jung (1875–1961) was a Swiss doctor who in the 20th century established the discipline known as analytical psychology. Though Jung was a respected scientist, he spent much of his life studying alchemy, astrology, and the occult. In his writings, Jung uses some of the symbols and terminology of alchemy to represent various stages in psychoanalysis.

many did. For example, during his lifetime the mathematician and alchemist John Dee (1527–1608) worked for both Queen Elizabeth of England and Emperor Rudolf II of the Holy Roman Empire in central Europe. Dee was considered one of the best educated men of his time, and he taught navigation to many of the English sailors who explored the coast of North America during the 16th century. Similarly, Lord Rosenberg, a wealthy count from Bohemia, was the patron of one of Dee's alchemist associates, Sir Edward Kelley.

By the start of the eighteenth century, the practice of alchemy had greatly declined in importance. It would soon be completely replaced by chemistry and other sciences that use experiments to better understand the natural world. Today, only a few people who are interested in the occult or magic still read or believe in the writings of Medieval alchemists.

MAGIC AND POPULAR CULTURE

Many people remain fascinated by the idea of magic, or of stories about powerful sorcerers using spells to battle magical creatures. The most popular movie at the start of 2015 was *The Hobbit: The Battle of the Five Armies*, the third installment of a series of films based on the fantasy literature of J.R.R. Tolkien. Tolkien's story features the wizard Gandalf, who uses his magic to help a band of adventurers defeat a powerful dragon, recover his treasure, and then defeat an army of enemy creatures.

The Hobbit films were directed by Australian Peter Jackson, who had previously adapted Tolkien's Lord of the Rings trilogy for the screen in 2001–2003. Chronicling the epic quest of a group of heroes to defeat the forces of an evil sorcerer and restore peace to the mythical land of Middle-Earth, the Lord of the Rings trilogy was a massive success, earning more than $3 billion worldwide.

Many other books and movies about wizards and magic have captured the interest of young people in recent years. The Harry Potter franchise, based on books by British author J.K. Rowling, included seven best-selling books and eight blockbuster movie adaptations. In

The fantasy genre of literature and movies, which often features magical creatures and powerful spell-casting wizards, remains extremely popular in the 21st century.

Rupert Grint, Daniel Radcliffe, and Emma Watson, stars of the popular Harry Potter series of films, pose with their wands at a promotional event.

the books and films, Harry and his friends Ron Weasley and Hermione Granger are students at the Hogwarts School of Witchcraft and Wizardry, and must use spells and magic powers to battle assorted evildoers, including a powerful sorcerer named Lord Voldemort. To date, the books have sold more than 450 million copies, while the films collectively have earned over $7.7 billion.

Clearly, magic and the supernatural never go out of style, particularly among young people. Teenagers seem to crave stories based on wizards, witches, and magical creatures. But this is not a new phenomenon; throughout history, magicians and magic have always had an important place in the world of entertainment.

MAGIC IN LITERATURE

The epic poem *The Odyssey*, written in the eighth century BCE, features numerous uses of magic and the supernatural. At one point the Greek hero Odysseus and his men land on an island ruled by Circe, a powerful sorceress. She uses her magic wand to turn his men into pigs, but Odysseus is protected by an herb that keeps him safe. However, the hero must live with her for a year before she finally makes his men human again and sets them free. When Odysseus is preparing to leave, Circe tells him how to perform a magical ritual that will enable him to speak with the spirits of the dead, who can explain to him how to return to his home. The character of Circe would reappear in other Greek and Roman mythology

The only surviving example of a complete fictional novel from the Roman Empire is *The Metamorphoses of Apuleius*. It was written around 160 CE, and describes a man named Lucius who wants to practice magic. While trying a spell, he accidentally transforms himself into a donkey. The book is about his travels as a donkey, through which Lucius learns more about the troubles of slaves and common people. Lucius eventually is returned to human form when he joins the cult of Isis, a mystery religion that was popular in the Roman Empire at the time.

Between the eleventh and fifteenth centuries, the kingdoms of Europe and the West were often at war with neighboring Muslim empires. Despite the fighting, there was an important exchange of knowledge between the two civilizations, and many writings by Roman and Greek philosophers that had been lost during the Dark Ages were re-introduced by Arab scholars. Some of these, such as the writings attributed to Hermes Trismegistus, increased interest in magic. A major influence on Western literature was the *Arabian Nights*, a collection of stories from Persia and Arabia. Several of the tales featured evil sorcerers, as well as other fantastic creatures such as djinn that could use magic to grant wishes.

During the Medieval period, a German legend arose about Doctor Faust, a successful scholar and alchemist who is frustrated by the limits of his knowledge. He makes a pact with a demon, trading his soul in exchange for unlimited knowledge and worldly pleasures. The story has been retold many times. One of the most famous versions is the play *The Tragical History of Doctor Faustus* (ca. 1592) by the English playwright Christopher Marlowe, a contemporary of Shakespeare. Two centuries later, the German playwright Johann Wolfgang von Goethe would compose a long, two-part version of the Faust story that is considered his masterwork. The story has also been adopted as an opera. German writer Thomas Mann's 1947 novel *Doktor Faustus* is a modern retelling of the story.

THE RISE OF THE FANTASY GENRE

During the 20th century, a new type of literature began to appear, featuring brave warriors and powerful magicians who struggled for power in worlds that were much different from reality. These worlds were filled with unusual creatures and monsters, and characterized by powerful magic that could be used to attack enemies or build empires. These types of stories came to be called fantasy literature.

Two of the most popular writers of this genre were friends and colleagues from the United Kingdom, J.R.R. Tolkien and C.S. Lewis. Tolkien, a professor at Oxford University, wrote about a land called Middle-Earth, which was populated by elves, dwarves, small creatures called hobbits, evil orcs, and humans. Good and evil characters wage war for control of the land. Among the leaders of the good side are several described as wizards. One of them, Gandalf, plays a key role in the story. Unlike most wizards in literature, Gandalf carries a sword and uses it in battle. He is a mentor and friend to the main characters in Tolkien's novel for children, *The Hobbit* (1937), as well as his most famous work, the three books of the Lord of the Rings trilogy, which were published in the 1950s. Tolkien later expanded on the mythology of Middle-Earth in *The Silmarillion* (1977) and other works.

Like Tolkien, C.S. Lewis was a professor at Oxford University, though he later taught at Cambridge University as well. Lewis was well known for his books and essays about Christianity, but his most famous work was a seven-volume series for children that has become known as the Chronicles of Narnia. Several of the books feature powerful sorcerers, including *The Lion, The Witch, and The Wardrobe* (1950), in which a powerful spellcaster imposes an eternal winter on the fantasy land known as Narnia. Interestingly, most of the magic-using characters in the Narnia books are evil women.

The Lord of the Rings trilogy and the Chronicles of Narnia inspired many other fantasy writers, such as Ursula Le Guin, Anne McCaffrey, Piers Anthony, T.H. White, Fritz Leiber, and Terry Brooks. They also inspired J.K. Rowling, who wrote the popular Harry Potter series of books in the 1990s and early 2000s.

The sword-wielding wizard Gandalf and two of his companions in a scene from the third Lord of the Rings film, The Return of the King *(2003). Since being published in the mid-1950s, J.R.R. Tolkien's books have been translated into dozens of languages, have sold more than 150 million copies, and were turned into a wildly profitable series of films.*

The popularity of fantasy literature inspired a role-playing game that would become very popular in the 1980s: Dungeons & Dragons. D&D, as it was often called, enabled players to create their own characters, such as fighters, magic-users, clerics, or thieves, and control them in adventures intended to fight unusual monsters and find fantastic treasures. Magic-users had the ability to cast spells to help their parties, while clerics were religious leaders whose deities could grant them certain magical powers, such as the ability to heal injured companions or to make undead monsters like ghouls or vampires go away.

In recent years video games utilizing fantasy themes of "swords and sorcery" have become very popular, such as *World of Warcraft* or *The Elder Scrolls.*

It is clear that magic and the supernatural will continue to fascinate young people, even as scientists and inventors in our modern age develop new technologies, such as 3D printing and quantum mechanics, that appear to the uneducated to be truly magical.

CHRONOLOGY

495 BCE   Death of Pythagoras of Samos, a mathematician and philosopher who some ancient Greeks worshiped as a powerful magician.

322 BCE   The Greek philosopher Aristotle dies. His writings on astronomy and the properties of the natural world would have a powerful influence on Medieval scholarship.

172 BCE   The name Hermes Trismegistus appears in the records of an Egyptian temple. Writings attributed to Hermes Trismegistus explained that there is a world of supernatural magic that could be drawn upon by those who gained enough knowledge.

380 CE   Christianity becomes the official religion of the Roman Empire. In subsequent centuries the government and Church would take steps to eliminate mystery religions.

476   Fall of the Roman Empire, after which the Christian Church holds significant political power in Europe.

1155   Death of the Welsh cleric Geoffrey of Monmouth, who wrote about the wizard Merlin in his stories about King Arthur. Merlin would become the archetype for the wizard in literature as a wise and powerful counselor.

1320   Roman Catholic Pope John XXII authorizes the Inquisition to began persecuting sorcerers and witches.

1440   Serial murderer Gilles de Rais is tried and executed for sorcery in France.

1558   The wizard and alchemist John Dee becomes an advisor to Queen Elizabeth II of England.

1663	Alchemist Robert Boyle becomes a member of the Royal Society, an important scientific organization in Great Britain. Boyle would become known for his accomplishments in the field of chemistry.
1727	After the death of renowned scientist Sir Isaac Newton, it is discovered that he had secretly practiced alchemy.
1887	The magical organization Hermetic Order of the Golden Dawn is founded.
1917	The most famous of the stage magicians, Harry Houdini, becomes president of the Society of American Magicians.
1923	Aleister Crowley becomes the leader of Ordo Templi Orientis, a magical organization. His teachings would have an enormous impact on 20th and 21st century occultists and neopagans.
1949	Gerald Gardner's first book, *High Magic's Aid*, is published. Gardner would become a key figure in the history of Wicca, or modern witchcraft, the most popular of the neopagan religions today.
1997	The book *Harry Potter and the Philosopher's Stone* is published in Great Britain. It is the first in a series of highly popular books about young wizards.
2014	In Saudi Arabia, an older woman is convicted of sorcery and executed.
2015	The fantasy film *The Hobbit: The Battle of the Five Armies*, featuring the wizard Gandalf, is one of the most popular films of the year.

GLOSSARY

alchemy—a pseudoscience based on the belief that materials can be changed or transformed through supernatural means. As natural laws became better understood, alchemy was eventually replaced by chemistry and other modern scientific disciplines.

amulet—an object that is believed to have the power to protect its possessor from harm.

animism—a belief that all things in nature, including plants, animals, and natural features such as rocks and rivers, have a spirit, and that humans can communicate with the spirits through magical rituals. Most traditional religions of indigenous peoples are animist in nature.

astrology—the study of how the movement and position of celestial bodies, such as stars and planets, influence human affairs and the natural world.

cleric—a member of a religious organization, such as a priest.

crucible—a ceramic or metal container in which metals or other substances may be melted or subjected to very high temperatures.

cult—a system of religious veneration and devotion directed toward a particular person or object.

deity—a god or goddess.

demonology—the study of demons.

Druid—a religious leader in the ancient Celtic tribes who was believed to have magical powers.

fantasy—a category of fiction that often involves mythical themes and characters, including dragons, wizards with magical powers, and sword-wielding heroes.

folklore—traditional beliefs, legends, and customs of a people.

grimoire—a book of ancient knowledge that includes spells and instructions for magical rituals.

hallucination—when a person hears, sees, or otherwise senses things that don't exist, or that others can't perceive.

hekau—an ancient Egyptian magician.

Hermetic—relating to an ancient occult tradition, based on writings attributed to the Greek philosopher Hermes Trismegistus, that included alchemy, astrology, and theurgy, or the use of magic.

incantation—a chant or spell that uses words.

incense—a gum residue from plants that when burned emits a sweet aroma. It is often used in religious services.

indigenous people—people who originated in or are native to a particular region or country.

Inquisition—a period of European history spanning some 400 years in which officials of the Roman Catholic Church used cruel methods, often involving torture, to investigate suspected cases of sorcery or occult practices.

Medieval—referring to an era in European history that began around year 500 CE and lasted until the start of the Renaissance around 1500 CE. This period is also known as the Middle Ages.

medium—a person who is believed to be able to communicate with the spirit world.

metallurgy—the study of metals and how they can be produced or combined to create alloys with different physical properties.

necromancy—the practice of contacting the dead in order to request their aid or counsel.

neopagan—a person who practices paganism in the modern world.

New Age—a modern quasi-religious movement that often includes a belief in magic and combines practices like astrology, paganism, and alternative medicine.

occult—belief in the supernatural world, or magical beliefs, practices, and phenomena related to that world.

paranormal—events or activities that cannot be explained or understood by natural or scientific laws.

shaman—the spiritual leader of an indigenous community, who is believed to be able to heal people and see the future through his or her interactions with the spirit world. Sometimes called a medicine man.

sorcery—magic that is used to harm or kill a person, or to destroy property. Also known as "black magic."

supernatural—related to forces beyond the normal world; magical or miraculous.

theurgy—human interaction with the gods or the spirit world through the use of magic.

vision quest—a personal, spiritual search undertaken by Native Americans in order to learn about the future through a trance or vision.

wizard—a word derived from the Old English *wys*, meaning "wise," and denoting an educated person or counselor. Use of the word wizard to describe someone proficient in magic and the occult originated in the 1400s, when philosophy became interwoven with a belief in Hermetic magic. In the modern day, a wizard is someone who excels at a particular discipline.

FURTHER READING

Billings, Arlene, and Beryl Dhanjal. *Supernatural Signs, Symbols, and Codes*. New York: Rosen, 2011.

Booth, Mark. *The Sacred History: How Angels, Mystics and Higher Intelligence Made Our World*. New York: Atria Books, 2013.

Davies, Owen. *Grimoires: A History of Magic Books*. New York: Oxford University Press, 2009.

Freke, Timothy, and Peter Gandy. *The Hermetica: The Lost Wisdom of the Pharaohs*. New York: Putnam, 1999.

Hauck, Dennis W. *Sorcerer's Stone: A Beginner's Guide to Alchemy*. Sacramento, Calif.: Crucible Books, 2013.

Lawrence-Mathers, Anne. *Magic and Medieval Society*. New York: Routledge, 2014.

Long, Carolyn Morrow. *Spiritual Merchants: Religion, Magic, and Commerce*. Knoxville: University of Tennessee Press, 2001.

Roland, Paul. *The Dark History of the Occult: Magic, Madness and Murder*. London: Arcturus Publishing, 2011.

INTERNET RESOURCES

http://hermetic.com

The Hermetic Library includes links to a collection of texts and sites relating to Hermeticism, the occult, and the beliefs of Aleister Crowley.

www.themiddleages.net/life/magic.html

This website on the history of the Medieval period includes a page on magical beliefs and practices.

http://oto-usa.org

Official website for the U.S. grand lodge of Ordo Templi Orientis, a magical organization founded in the late nineteenth century.

www.lloydlibrary.org/exhibits/alchemy/index.html

The Lloyd Library and Museum in Cincinnati provides this page on the history of alchemy, with links related to magical beliefs and practices.

http://www.shamanism.com

This website provides information on what shamans do and how they heal people through their magic and rituals.

Publisher's Note: The websites listed on this page were active at the time of publication. The publisher is not responsible for websites that have changed their address or discontinued operation since the date of publication. The publisher reviews and updates the websites each time the book is reprinted.

www.pbs.org/wgbh/nova/physics/newton-alchemist-new-man.html

This companion website to the PBS program NOVA includes information about Sir Isaac Newton's covert practice of alchemy in the 17th century.

www.dynionmwyn.net/PaganPage/intro.html

Visitors can learn about pagan traditions, history and legal rights at the website maintained by the Georgia-based Universal Federation of Pagans.

www.cog.org

The international Wicca organization Covenant of the Goddess maintains an Internet page that features information about Wicca history and practices.

www.witchway.net

Assorted rituals and spells of neopagans can be found at this Internet site.

www.pantheon.org

The *Encyclopedia Mythica* is a good starting place if you are doing research on mythology and related topics.

INDEX

Numbers in **bold italic** refer to captions.

ABOUT
THE AUTHOR

Dorothy Kavanaugh is the author of many books for young people, including *Judaism, Christianity, Islam* (Mason Crest, 2004), *A Girl's/Guy's Guide to Conflict* (Enslow, 2008), and *Infamous Terrorists* (Eldorado Ink, 2012). She is a graduate of Bryn Mawr College and lives with her family in the suburbs of Philadelphia.